Monday

Tuesday

Wednesday

Thursday

Friday

Saturday

Sunday

Places to Go

People to See

Things to Do

Special Reminders

Monday	

Tuesday	

Wednesday	

Thursday	

Friday	

Saturday	

Sunday	

Places to Go

☐
☐
☐
☐
☐
☐

People to See

☐
☐
☐
☐
☐
☐

Things to Do

☐
☐
☐
☐
☐
☐
☐
☐
☐
☐
☐
☐
☐
☐

Special Reminders

☐
☐
☐
☐
☐
☐
☐

Monday

Tuesday

Wednesday

Thursday

Friday

Saturday

Sunday

Places to Go

People to See

Things to Do

Special Reminders

Monday	

Tuesday	

Wednesday	

Thursday	

Friday	

Saturday	

Sunday	

Places to Go

☐ _______________________
☐ _______________________
☐ _______________________
☐ _______________________
☐ _______________________
☐ _______________________

People to See

☐ _______________________
☐ _______________________
☐ _______________________
☐ _______________________
☐ _______________________
☐ _______________________

Things to Do

☐ _______________________
☐ _______________________
☐ _______________________
☐ _______________________
☐ _______________________
☐ _______________________
☐ _______________________
☐ _______________________
☐ _______________________
☐ _______________________
☐ _______________________
☐ _______________________

Special Reminders

☐ _______________________
☐ _______________________
☐ _______________________
☐ _______________________
☐ _______________________
☐ _______________________
☐ _______________________

Monday

Tuesday

Wednesday

Thursday

Friday

Saturday

Sunday

Places to Go

☐
☐
☐
☐
☐
☐
☐

People to See

☐
☐
☐
☐
☐

Things to Do

☐
☐
☐
☐
☐
☐
☐
☐
☐
☐
☐
☐
☐
☐

Special Reminders

☐
☐
☐
☐
☐
☐
☐

Monday	

Places to Go

☐ _______________
☐ _______________
☐ _______________
☐ _______________
☐ _______________
☐ _______________

Tuesday	

People to See

☐ _______________
☐ _______________
☐ _______________
☐ _______________
☐ _______________
☐ _______________

Wednesday	

Things to Do

☐ _______________
☐ _______________
☐ _______________
☐ _______________
☐ _______________
☐ _______________
☐ _______________
☐ _______________
☐ _______________
☐ _______________
☐ _______________
☐ _______________
☐ _______________
☐ _______________
☐ _______________
☐ _______________

Thursday	

Friday	

Saturday	

Special Reminders

☐ _______________
☐ _______________
☐ _______________
☐ _______________
☐ _______________
☐ _______________
☐ _______________

Sunday	

Monday	
Tuesday	
Wednesday	
Thursday	
Friday	
Saturday	
Sunday	

Places to Go

People to See

Things to Do

Special Reminders

| **Monday** | |

| **Tuesday** | |

| **Wednesday** | |

| **Thursday** | |

| **Friday** | |

| **Saturday** | |

| **Sunday** | |

Places to Go

People to See

Things to Do

Special Reminders

Monday

Tuesday

Wednesday

Thursday

Friday

Saturday

Sunday

Places to Go

People to See

Things to Do

Special Reminders

| **Monday** | |

| **Tuesday** | |

| **Wednesday** | |

| **Thursday** | |

| **Friday** | |

| **Saturday** | |

| **Sunday** | |

Places to Go

People to See

Things to Do

Special Reminders

Monday

Tuesday

Wednesday

Thursday

Friday

Saturday

Sunday

Places to Go

People to See

Things to Do

Special Reminders

| **Monday** | |

| **Tuesday** | |

| **Wednesday** | |

| **Thursday** | |

| **Friday** | |

| **Saturday** | |

| **Sunday** | |

Places to Go

People to See

Things to Do

Special Reminders

Monday

Tuesday

Wednesday

Thursday

Friday

Saturday

Sunday

Places to Go

People to See

Things to Do

Special Reminders

Monday

Tuesday

Wednesday

Thursday

Friday

Saturday

Sunday

Places to Go

People to See

Things to Do

Special Reminders

Monday

Tuesday

Wednesday

Thursday

Friday

Saturday

Sunday

Places to Go

People to See

Things to Do

Special Reminders

Monday

Tuesday

Wednesday

Thursday

Friday

Saturday

Sunday

Places to Go

People to See

Things to Do

Special Reminders

Monday

Tuesday

Wednesday

Thursday

Friday

Saturday

Sunday

Places to Go

People to See

Things to Do

Special Reminders

Monday

Tuesday

Wednesday

Thursday

Friday

Saturday

Sunday

Places to Go

People to See

Things to Do

Special Reminders

Monday	

Tuesday	

Wednesday	

Thursday	

Friday	

Saturday	

Sunday	

Places to Go

☐
☐
☐
☐
☐
☐

People to See

☐
☐
☐
☐
☐
☐

Things to Do

☐
☐
☐
☐
☐
☐
☐
☐
☐
☐
☐
☐
☐

Special Reminders

☐
☐
☐
☐
☐
☐
☐

Monday	Places to Go

Tuesday	People to See

Wednesday	Things to Do

Thursday

Friday

Saturday

Special Reminders

Sunday

Monday

Tuesday

Wednesday

Thursday

Friday

Saturday

Sunday

Places to Go

People to See

Things to Do

Special Reminders

| **Monday** | Places to Go |

| **Tuesday** |

| **Wednesday** | People to See |

| **Thursday** | Things to Do |

| **Friday** |

| **Saturday** |

Special Reminders

| **Sunday** |

Monday	

Tuesday	

Wednesday	

Thursday	

Friday	

Saturday	

Sunday	

Places to Go

People to See

Things to Do

Special Reminders

Monday	

Tuesday	

Wednesday	

Thursday	

Friday	

Saturday	

Sunday	

Places to Go

People to See

Things to Do

Special Reminders

| **Monday** | |

| **Tuesday** | |

| **Wednesday** | |

| **Thursday** | |

| **Friday** | |

| **Saturday** | |

| **Sunday** | |

Places to Go

People to See

Things to Do

Special Reminders

Monday		Places to Go

| **Tuesday** | | People to See |

| **Wednesday** | | |

| **Thursday** | | Things to Do |

| **Friday** | | |

| **Saturday** | | Special Reminders |

| **Sunday** | | |

Monday

Tuesday

Wednesday

Thursday

Friday

Saturday

Sunday

Places to Go

People to See

Things to Do

Special Reminders

| **Monday** | |

| **Tuesday** | |

| **Wednesday** | |

| **Thursday** | |

| **Friday** | |

| **Saturday** | |

| **Sunday** | |

Places to Go

People to See

Things to Do

Special Reminders

Monday

Tuesday

Wednesday

Thursday

Friday

Saturday

Sunday

Places to Go

People to See

Things to Do

Special Reminders

Monday	

Tuesday	

Wednesday	

Thursday	

Friday	

Saturday	

Sunday	

Places to Go

People to See

Things to Do

Special Reminders

Monday

Tuesday

Wednesday

Thursday

Friday

Saturday

Sunday

Places to Go

People to See

Things to Do

Special Reminders

| **Monday** | |

| **Tuesday** | |

| **Wednesday** | |

| **Thursday** | |

| **Friday** | |

| **Saturday** | |

| **Sunday** | |

Places to Go

☐
☐
☐
☐
☐
☐
☐

People to See

☐
☐
☐
☐
☐
☐
☐

Things to Do

☐
☐
☐
☐
☐
☐
☐
☐
☐
☐
☐
☐
☐

Special Reminders

☐
☐
☐
☐
☐
☐
☐
☐

Monday

Tuesday

Wednesday

Thursday

Friday

Saturday

Sunday

Places to Go

People to See

Things to Do

Special Reminders

Monday	

Tuesday	

Wednesday	

Thursday	

Friday	

Saturday	

Sunday	

Places to Go

☐ __________________
☐ __________________
☐ __________________
☐ __________________
☐ __________________
☐ __________________

People to See

☐ __________________
☐ __________________
☐ __________________
☐ __________________
☐ __________________
☐ __________________

Things to Do

☐ __________________
☐ __________________
☐ __________________
☐ __________________
☐ __________________
☐ __________________
☐ __________________
☐ __________________
☐ __________________
☐ __________________
☐ __________________
☐ __________________
☐ __________________

Special Reminders

☐ __________________
☐ __________________
☐ __________________
☐ __________________
☐ __________________
☐ __________________

<table>
<tr><td>

Monday

Tuesday

Wednesday

Thursday

Friday

Saturday

Sunday

</td><td>

Places to Go

☐
☐
☐
☐
☐
☐

People to See

☐
☐
☐
☐
☐
☐

Things to Do

☐
☐
☐
☐
☐
☐
☐
☐
☐
☐
☐
☐
☐

Special Reminders

☐
☐
☐
☐
☐
☐
☐

</td></tr>
</table>

Monday	

Tuesday	

Wednesday	

Thursday	

Friday	

Saturday	

Sunday	

Places to Go

- ☐
- ☐
- ☐
- ☐
- ☐
- ☐

People to See

- ☐
- ☐
- ☐
- ☐
- ☐
- ☐

Things to Do

- ☐
- ☐
- ☐
- ☐
- ☐
- ☐
- ☐
- ☐
- ☐
- ☐
- ☐
- ☐
- ☐
- ☐

Special Reminders

- ☐
- ☐
- ☐
- ☐
- ☐
- ☐

Monday

Tuesday

Wednesday

Thursday

Friday

Saturday

Sunday

Places to Go

People to See

Things to Do

Special Reminders

Monday	

Tuesday	

Wednesday	

Thursday	

Friday	

Saturday	

Sunday	

Places to Go

People to See

Things to Do

Special Reminders

Monday

Tuesday

Wednesday

Thursday

Friday

Saturday

Sunday

Places to Go

People to See

Things to Do

Special Reminders

Monday

Tuesday

Wednesday

Thursday

Friday

Saturday

Sunday

Places to Go

People to See

Things to Do

Special Reminders

Monday

Tuesday

Wednesday

Thursday

Friday

Saturday

Sunday

Places to Go

People to See

Things to Do

Special Reminders

Monday

Tuesday

Wednesday

Thursday

Friday

Saturday

Sunday

Places to Go

People to See

Things to Do

Special Reminders

Monday

Tuesday

Wednesday

Thursday

Friday

Saturday

Sunday

Places to Go

People to See

Things to Do

Special Reminders

<table>
<tr><td>

Monday

Tuesday

Wednesday

Thursday

Friday

Saturday

Sunday

</td><td>

Places to Go

☐
☐
☐
☐
☐
☐

People to See

☐
☐
☐
☐
☐
☐

Things to Do

☐
☐
☐
☐
☐
☐
☐
☐
☐
☐
☐
☐
☐
☐

Special Reminders

☐
☐
☐
☐
☐
☐
☐
☐

</td></tr>
</table>

Monday

Tuesday

Wednesday

Thursday

Friday

Saturday

Sunday

Places to Go

People to See

Things to Do

Special Reminders

Monday		Places to Go

| **Tuesday** | |

| **Wednesday** | | People to See |

| **Thursday** | | Things to Do |

| **Friday** | |

| **Saturday** | | Special Reminders |

| **Sunday** | |

Monday

Tuesday

Wednesday

Thursday

Friday

Saturday

Sunday

Places to Go

People to See

Things to Do

Special Reminders

Monday

Tuesday

Wednesday

Thursday

Friday

Saturday

Sunday

Places to Go

People to See

Things to Do

Special Reminders

<table>
<tr><td>

Monday

Tuesday

Wednesday

Thursday

Friday

Saturday

Sunday

</td><td>

Places to Go

☐
☐
☐
☐
☐
☐

People to See

☐
☐
☐
☐
☐
☐

Things to Do

☐
☐
☐
☐
☐
☐
☐
☐
☐
☐
☐
☐
☐

Special Reminders

☐
☐
☐
☐
☐
☐

</td></tr>
</table>

Monday	
Tuesday	
Wednesday	
Thursday	
Friday	
Saturday	
Sunday	

Places to Go

☐
☐
☐
☐
☐
☐
☐

People to See

☐
☐
☐
☐
☐
☐

Things to Do

☐
☐
☐
☐
☐
☐
☐
☐
☐
☐
☐
☐
☐
☐

Special Reminders

☐
☐
☐
☐
☐
☐
☐

Monday

Tuesday

Wednesday

Thursday

Friday

Saturday

Sunday

Places to Go

People to See

Things to Do

Special Reminders

Monday

Tuesday

Wednesday

Thursday

Friday

Saturday

Sunday

Places to Go

People to See

Things to Do

Special Reminders